# Missionary Stories from Around the World

# Missionary Stories from Around the World

## Betty Swinford

CF4·K

Copyright © 2005 Betty Swinford
This edition printed in 2009
Reprinted in 2013 and 2015
ISBN 978-1-84550-564-6

Previously published under
ISBN 1-84550-042-3

Published by Christian Focus Publications
Geanies House, Fearn, Tain, Ross-shire
IV20 1TW, Scotland, Great Britain
www.christianfocus.com
email:info@christianfocus.com

Cover design Daniel van Straaten
Black and white illustrations by Stuart Mingham

Printed and bound by Nørhaven, Denmark

Scripture quotations are taken from the King James
Version of the Bible.

# Contents

# Where do you want to go?

# A Daring Venture

In the thick rainforest, hidden from the world, lived a tribe of Indians known as the Aucas, which means "savage". The Aucas were very violent. In fact, even their headhunting neighbours, the Jivaro tribe, were afraid of them.

In 1955, four missionaries from the United States felt called by God to preach the Gospel to the Aucas. One of these missionaries was Nate Saint. He was thirty-two years old and a pilot. Having learned to fly in high school, Nate flew during World War II. Now, he had joined the Missionary Aviation Fellowship and it was his job to fly medicine, mail, and other supplies to missionaries.

By scouting the area in his plane, Nate discovered an Auca settlement only fifteen minutes from the mission station. Nate and three other missionaries began to plan a way to reach the Aucas. It would be very secretive because if the outside world found out and tried to gain access to the tribe, it would ruin everything. The outsiders would be killed and the missionaries would never be able to contact the savages. As it was, the only person who could help them was an Auca girl who had left the tribe and was living with Nate's sister, Rachel.

Nate found that if he flew over the Auca village in a tight circle, he could then lower gifts and keep them almost perfectly still until the natives had taken the gifts. Then on the fourth night, the missionaries spoke to the Aucas through a loudspeaker system. It was not long until the natives began bringing gifts to the missionaries – parrots, cooked fish, and wooden combs.

It surely did seem like a real friendship was forming between the Aucas and the missionaries.

Finally, Nate found a place where he could safely land the small plane. It was a long, sandy beach by the Auca village. He would land and leave gifts as a sign of friendship.

One day, Nate landed the plane and along with four other missionaries, made camp. At first, the Aucas seemed very frightened. Nate flew the plane over their village several times and dropped gifts, then landed again.

Then one man, a woman, and a girl came to their camp. It was Friday afternoon and the visit seemed friendly but after a few hours, they suddenly got up and hurried away. The next day, no one came at all. Nate flew over the village, dropping gifts, which seemed to take away their fears.

However, on the afternoon of January 8, 1956, spears suddenly began to fly and all the missionaries were killed.

There had been a lookout in a tree house and he had sensed no danger so the attack had come as a complete surprise. More than twenty pilots from the United States immediately offered to come and take Nate's place.

Much later, one of the Aucas explained why he had helped murder the missionaries. He said they could not understand why white men wanted to be friends so they became suspicious. They did not know how, but in some way, they believed it was all a trap. After the killings, they realized their mistake but of course, it was too late. A search party found the missionaries the next day but there were no signs of a struggle. That is how they knew the attack had been a surprise to the missionaries.

Nate Saint was born in 1923 and always loved to fly. He was martyred in 1956 on January 8, a Sunday afternoon and was only 33 years old.

All the men were buried at the campsite where they had given their lives trying to bring the message of salvation to the tribe of savages.

Why did Nate Saint have to die such an awful death when he was doing something so good and noble? Did it make any kind of sense? We will find out in the next story.

*"Precious in the sight of the LORD is the death of his saints" (Psalm 116:15).*

# Living with the Aucas

Jim Elliot was one of the five missionaries who was speared to death by the Auca tribe. As a tribe they were violent and even inspired fear in the other local tribes people. Some of the other tribes thought they were cannibals.

Jim's wife, Elisabeth, even in her sorrow over her husband's death, loved the Aucas just because Jim loved them. However, should she risk her life and that of her tiny child, Valerie, to try to carry on the work of trying to reach this heathen tribe? She had to be sure that she was following God's will.

She and Jim had been working among the Quichua Indians in a place called Shandia in Ecuador for a while. However, it was when she was invited to the home of some friends that God gave her the answer. Three Auca women appeared and she knew she must work among them, even though the danger would be great.

Elisabeth became friends with two of the women. Their names were Mintaka and Mankamu. After a while, they wanted to take her to their Auca village. Friends thought she was crazy even to consider such a thing.

Thinking of her husband, Jim, who had been speared by the savages, she asked the women,

16

"Will they kill us? Will they spear us?" She had to be sure for to her, the word "Auca" meant death.

The Auca women promised they would not kill them. They would explain to their people that the white people were good and could be trusted.

God gave her several scriptures to comfort her. One was, *"I do not fear what man can do unto me. The Lord is on my side to help me."*

It was discouraging though when they heard that a Quichua man named Honorio had just been speared by the Aucas. He had eighteen spears in his body and his dog had three.

However, God promised to protect them. They started out, three-year-old Valerie, Rachel Saint (Nate's sister), Elisabeth, and their carriers. Valerie was carried in a little wooden chair. The last of the journey was made by canoe and when they reached what was called the strong city, they saw people who wore no clothes. Their hair was cut straight across the forehead but long in the back. Their eyebrows had been plucked or shaved off. They were now in one of the most savage tribes on Earth but they were in the hands of God. He would not fail them.

The houses were only poles with leaf roofs and no walls. The Quichua who had come with them made Rachel and Elisabeth tables to work on since it was their goal to put the Auca language on paper. They even gave Elisabeth a nickname - Gikair - meaning "woodpecker") There was no furniture other than the table and Valerie's bed made from bamboo. Elisabeth slept in a hammock. This she could use as a bed, chair, or stool.

Each house had a fire going twenty-four hours a day. The Aucas slept with their feet near the fire for the nights were chilly. You could even cook on the fires from your hammock without ever getting up.

In the mornings, the men would go out hunting with their blowguns and spears. They hunted monkeys, squirrels, toucans, and parrots. Fish was also a great part of their diet. They had no stools but squatted and worked from the ground. They ate huge meals of cooked fish, plantain (a plant with basil leaves and tiny green flowers) and manioc (root vegetable). To smoke fish, they would collect green sticks and place them over the fire. Then, they would put the fish on them, covering them with green leaves. When they cooked a monkey, they ate the tail, head, eyes, ears, and brain. A certain type of squirrel

19

too was completely eaten, especially the stomach and whatever was in it.

Every spare moment was given to studying the language, trying to find ways to form it and then transform it into words. Sometimes, the backs of the white women hurt from sitting without support. Only little Valerie was totally happy and content. She had her bed, her doll, and its blanket. The Aucas loved her and gave her lots of attention.

In return, she shared with the Aucas her picture books, crayons and colouring books, and even the grown-up natives loved to colour. Valerie loved the jungle, her Indian playmates, and she never missed her toys.

They lived with the Aucas for two years. Elisabeth got some of the language down on paper. Today, many of the Aucas have accepted

Christ and are now telling others about their wonderful Saviour and Lord.

*"So shall my word be that goeth forth out of my mouth: it shall not return unto me void, but it shall accomplish that which I please..." (Isaiah 55:11).*

# A Day of Small Things

In the country of Scotland a little boy wanted to give his heart to Jesus. In the middle of the church, in front of everyone, he kneeled down to pray and gave his life to Christ. One old man knelt down beside him and prayed with him but some of the others thought that this little fellow was very foolish. How could a four-year-old boy possibly understand about salvation and Jesus

Christ? It was for adults to understand these things.

However, what these men thought did not trouble the little lad as he belonged to Jesus now. What these men thought did not trouble God either as God loves little children to come to him. And he does not want anyone to stop them.

The little boy's name was Robert Moffat, but at that time, everyone called him "Robbie" and as the years began to pass, it was clear that Robbie did indeed know God and that God's hand was upon his life, leading and guiding him.

As a teenager, Robert left home and went to the town of High Leigh in England to work as an under-gardener. When he was there he joined the Methodists and grew strong spiritually. His love for God grew. He longed even more to serve him. No one questioned his salvation now.

One day while taking a walk, he saw a sign announcing a missionary meeting. It was at that moment when Robert Moffat decided to become a missionary – just from a small poster! When he was just twenty-one, he was in South Africa.

Travelling deep into Africa was very dangerous. What few roads there were had been washed out by rains. Many had died trying to reach the people of this continent. There were also many things to threaten and kill a person in an instant such as lions, crocodiles, and snakes. In addition, war-like natives were a danger too. Monkeys hooted, Jackals howled at night, and Hyenas crept around so slyly one could not be sure where they were.

Robert knew the dangers but his heart was set upon conquering all the difficulties. He also realised that men who knew the country well would never go where he went. The dangers were simply too great.

He learned about the country and the people, the way they lived, and their languages. The one thing that would make him a blessing to thousands and thousands of people.

In 1817, Robert went to the Kraal (village) and there the Chief, a murderer who terrified the people, gave his heart to Christ. For this evil man to even listen to the Gospel message, much less receive it was a miracle. However, God knows how to touch the most wicked heart because He loves them so much.

On that same trip, Robert met the Bechwanas. It was with these people that he would live for most of his missionary life in Africa.

On a visit to Cape Town, Robert met and married the woman who would work by his side in Africa for the next fifty-one years. Three of their children died as babies but five of them lived.

Robert Moffat made a path for other missionaries to travel as they spread the Word of God and saw thousands come to know Christ. He even translated the language of the Bechwanas and opened many mission stations. He served in an area of hundreds of miles.

After fifty-four years of serving the Lord in Africa, he and his wife retired and went to live in England. His wife died a year later, but Robert continued to help missions in any way he could for the rest of his life.

As you can see, what you do with your life does not have to start out as some great and glorious thing. It can begin with something very small like a four-year-old child that people thought could not possibly know what he was doing. Look at the boy David in the Old Testament. He was scorned by those who were older than him. They actually thought they were wiser too. However, David knew what God had put in his heart and although he was just a boy, he went out and killed Goliath and saved his people.

*"Though thy beginning was small, yet thy latter end should greatly increase" (Job 8:7).*

# Amma

This is the story of one of the most amazing women who ever lived, her name was Amy Carmichael. She was born in a time when women wore their dresses very full, had very narrow waistlines. Their dresses were so long that came all the way down to their high-topped, button shoes. Always a spiritual child, Amy prayed often and earnestly, "God, won't you please turn my brown eyes blue?" After many such prayers however, she decided she would have to live with those brown eyes.

Other times, she would lie in bed at night and with one hand, smooth the sheet beside her. At the same time, she would ask, "Please, Lord Jesus, come sit beside me while I go to sleep. Please talk to me."

God saw that there was somebody that he could use. She was devoted and loving. Most of all, she was devoted to God.

Amy Carmichael was born in Ireland in 1867. She was the eldest of seven children and heartbroken when her father died at a young age.

Her thoughts turned to the future and she wondered what God's plan was for her life. What could possibly lay ahead for her? She came out of church on a blustery cold, winter morning with her family. Glancing around, she saw a poor, tattered old woman struggling against the bitter cold, carrying a large bundle. She and her brothers stopped to stare but what Amy felt was sorrow and heartbreak. Amy was dressed in finery, while this wretched old woman was in tatters. Amy was ashamed of the fact that she felt embarrassed for the poor woman. She wanted to help but pride held her back.

The bitter cold swept the old woman's rags about her and a cold wind swept through Amy's heart.

Suddenly, as if someone were speaking to her, she heard these words, *"Now, if any man build upon this foundation gold, silver, precious stones, wood, hay, stubble, every man's work shall be made manifest : for the day shall declare it, because it shall be revealed by fire; and the fire shall try every man's work of what sort it is. If any man's work abide, which he hath built thereupon, he shall receive a reward" (1 Corinthians 3:12-14).*

At a conference in Glasgow, Scotland, Amy knew that God's hand was upon her life. Amy gladly accepted the call to serve the One who had given His life and His blood for her salvation.

Eventually, Amy was sent to India by a missionary society in England. There, she worked for her Saviour without ever returning to her native land. She never forgot about the tattered old woman with the big bundle and yearned to help those like her.

It was all so different though. The tom-tom drums beat all night and the blackness of the night was like something alive and threatening.

Then, she discovered the temple children. These children were young and given to the pagan temples. Men with evil minds could go to the temple and use these children in any way they chose.

Her heart broken and torn, Amy began taking the children and making a home for them. She was persecuted for her efforts but in the end, she rescued 1,000 children from the wicked things done to them. The children called her "Amma", which meant "Mother".

The world around her was dangerous and evil, *"Thou wilt keep him in perfect peace whose mind is stayed on thee,"* she told herself.

In one of her writings, she mentions an Indian girl named Mimosa. She said of Mimosa that "one look at Jesus and she was His forever, and she didn't even know His name." Mimosa belonged to Jesus forever, and she didn't even know His name. In some way, Jesus made Himself known to her and she would never be the same.

However over the years Amy grew ill and for the last twenty-two years of her life she ministered to her beloved India from a bed of suffering.

Amy's latter years make me think of the following verse in scripture.

*"Moses...choosing rather to suffer affliction with the people of God, than to enjoy the pleasures of sin for a season" (Hebrews 11:25).*

What does that mean? It means it's better to suffer for Christ than to go to all the fun parties and other fun stuff without ever giving God a thought. A life spent for Jesus has great rewards and in the end, eternal life.

# The Plodder

William Carey was born in 1761. In his mind, he saw himself doing great and mighty things. However, he did not see the suffering he would go through. There would be times when he made huge mistakes and other times he would succeed. One thing about William Carey, he would never give up!

He loved adventure but as a boy, he got a skin disease and it looked as if his dreams for adventure were gone. His parents believed that he would have to work indoors so William went to work as a shoe cobbler.

He gave his heart to Christ at an early age and when he was nineteen, he married Dorothy Placket who was twenty-five. He kept on working as a shoe cobbler and took a second job teaching school. He loved geography and to make the world come alive to his students, he took pieces of leather and made a globe.

Everything was going along fine until he felt the call of God to be a missionary. His wife rebelled. There were jungles in India, with lions, tigers, snakes, wild elephants, and natives that would kill without blinking an eye. There were also jungle sicknesses and malaria fever. His wife Dorothy was not interested in going to India.

Now, William may have been a small man and already bald but he was determined that Dorothy would go to India with him. In the end, he won!

They arrived in Calcutta in 1793 and were amazed to find people from all over the world. What a perfect place to begin their ministry.

However, his companion, Doctor Thomas, got them into trouble. He was the one who handled all their money but he was actually awful with money! To survive they were forced to take work on an indigo plantation.

A fever swept through the Carey family and their five-year-old son Peter died. Dorothy could not get over his death and the sorrow began to affect her mind. Every year, it got worse. William longed for one true earthly friend to whom he could turn at that time. He made God that friend and pressed more and more into the ministry he had come to India for in the first place.

More missionaries came to India but it was seven years before William saw his first convert. How discouraging that must have been. By 1821 though, the missionaries had baptized 1,400 new believers.

Still, India had very few missionaries so there was no one from whom William could learn. Because of this, he made many mistakes. On top of that, he had never been good at public speaking. Some called him "the Plodder" because he just kept plodding along anyway, never giving up. He still loved adventure and still wanted to reach the unsaved for Christ.

Meanwhile his wife had gone completely mad. While William was in the other room studying his Bible and preparing sermons, he tried to ignore her screaming. She finally died and William married again, sooner than the other missionaries thought he should. He would marry two more times in his life.

Though he was not the best at speaking, he was very good with languages. Although he had never had much education, by 1801 he had translated the New Testament into Bengali. Then, he tackled the Old Testament. After that, he and those who worked with him had translated parts of the Bible into more than forty different languages. He opened a Bible school so the natives of India could learn to be pastors, teachers, and missionaries. Twenty years later, there were 102 schools with close to 7,000 students.

However, William's great work was the Serampore College, which is still in operation today.

He had dreamed of doing great things for God and though he made many mistakes along the way, he did do great things.

William Carey died in 1834. He never went back to England. On his tombstone were the words — "A wretched, poor, and helpless worm. On thy kind arms I fall."

This sounds like the Apostle Paul. He was beaten, shipwrecked, stoned, and much more but he too was a plodder. He never gave up – he kept plodding along. The years of Dorothy's madness were dark for William but he was a victor even then.

*"I can do all things through Christ which strengtheneth me" (Philippians 4:13).*

# God Cannot Lie

Gladys Pierson stood at her mother's graveside in California, facing death for the first time in her teenage life. Where had her mother gone? What was life and death all about? What was the purpose of life?

Her father married again and Gladys and her new stepmother did not have a very good relationship. Still wondering what life was all about, she began visiting various churches. Most of them, however, were dull and lifeless until she stepped into one special church. There, she heard joyful singing and saw the glow on the faces of the teenagers. She was a little afraid but something was there, drawing her back. It wasn't long before she accepted Christ into her heart and felt the load of sin lift from her life.

As Gladys grew in spiritual things, she began to feel a stirring in her heart to spread God's word. She knew that when God calls a person to serve Him, He never looks at their age, wealth, colour, or anything else.

Gladys answered the call with gladness and became a world missionary. She travelled to many countries around the world, leading people to Christ.

However, people eventually grow tired and so did Gladys. She came back to California for a rest. She was going down a very steep flight of stairs to the basement for something when she tripped and fell. Bruised and battered, she was so crippled that she could not even get out of her bed.

Where was her calling now? Was she finished as a missionary? She began to search the Bible, looking for the answer. People in the churches where she had ministered prayed earnestly that she would recover. Her heart was in Jamaica, Hong Kong, and other parts of the world.

She did not get better. In great pain and sorrow, she found a scripture verse in Hebrews, *"...it was impossible for God to lie." (Hebrews 6:18)*

Gladys hung onto that verse like a drowning man clinging to a piece of driftwood. In her mind, she began quoting another verse. It was the very last part of Exodus 15:26 that said, *"I am the LORD that healeth thee."*

Lying in bed in agony she said aloud time after time, "I am the Lord that healeth thee ... God cannot lie. God cannot lie!"

People prayed and prayed, she prayed, the church prayed, but nothing happened. Then one Sunday night, still in bed and unable to move, she asked her pastor to have the church pray once more.

She was alone in the house when she felt an urge to place a foot on the floor. She did. There was no pain so she tried the other foot. Slowly, she stood up. She flexed her arms and legs – no pain. She walked around the room, smiling and rejoicing. The pain never came back. The God who cannot lie had kept His promise.

Now, what do you think Gladys did? What would you have done? Would you have been frightened about getting hurt again? Would you have been angry with God for not keeping you safe in the first place? Gladys was different. She remembered a newspaper article! 'Last summer in Florida, a shark bit off the arm of a teenager. Today, she is on the ocean surfing again, facing her fears and challenges with confidence.' "Lord, I want to be more like her," is what Gladys said.

We should thank God that Gladys was healed. However, God sometimes says no to our prayers. His thoughts can be different to ours. He might heal us by making our bodies better or he might heal us by giving us strength to carry on, working for him, despite our pain and problems.

God calls his followers "soldiers". Soldiers are sometimes shot but after they heal, they go back into battle. Hard times come to all of us but let us be soldiers and keep serving Christ. That is what Gladys did, she went back to the faraway places of the world to tell others about salvation through the precious blood of Jesus.

# Inn of Sixth Happiness

Do you kids want a story about adventure, danger, and suspense? Hold on then for this story has it all!

Gladys Aylward went to China as a missionary when she was twenty-six. She travelled by train, boat, bus, and mule. Finally, she made it to the mountains of Shansi – all this in spite of China and Russia being at war.

She settled in Yangchen and decided the best way to reach the people would be to set up an inn for caravans constantly coming by carrying iron, cotton, pots, and coal. However, the people were afraid of foreigners and the caravans went to other inns. Gladys boldly solved the problem. When she heard a caravan coming, she would go out to the road, grab the reins of the lead mule, and turn the caravan into their courtyard. The mules did not care as long as there was food and the muleteers followed the mules as there were warm beds and good food to be had. Their mules were well cared for too and Gladys had learned to speak their language pretty well so she told the men Bible stories. Things were going along very well. Then, disaster struck.

Her missionary companion, Mrs. Lawson, had a bad fall and died. Gladys was left alone in a foreign country. Her only help was from a Chinese Christian named Yang.

Gladys prayed for a way to reach the people, and the answer came in a most surprising way. You see, for many years the feet of baby girls had been tightly bound so they wouldn't grow. Now a law had been passed that the bindings must stop. But men could not go from house to house to remove the bindings. They needed a woman to do this, so they came to Gladys and offered her the job.

Gladys was delighted, for it meant that she could go into Chinese homes freely and without fear. It would be a great way to get the message of salvation to the people.

After two years in Yangchen a riot broke out in the prison. It was so bad that the soldiers were afraid to try and stop it. Again Gladys was called for. The warden challenged her, "You have been preaching that those who trust in Christ have nothing to fear. Now you go out there and stop this riot." Surely her heart was pounding as she entered the riot scene and tried to get the men to calm down. When they did, they told her what was troubling them. Returning to the warden, Gladys said, "No wonder they're rioting. They just want food and something to do."

After that the men were taught how to weave, and this gave them enough money to buy their food. It was the perfect solution to something that could have proved deadly.

The people gave Gladys the name Ai-weh-deh, or "The Virtuous" (Good Character).

Once she bought an unwanted child for nine pence and soon people began bringing other children to her. She welcomed them all without question.

In 1936, Gladys became a Chinese citizen. She wore the same type of clothing they wore and now, she was one of them.

Then came the war with the Japanese planes bombing the city of Yangchen and many people were killed. Those left alive fled into the mountains. The Japanese took the city of Yangchen, left, came back, then left again.

As the war continued, Gladys sometimes found herself behind enemy lines. She would gather information and get it back to the Chinese. In a way, she was a spy. It was dangerous but her faith was in God. A priest urged her to take her 100 children and flee. He sent her a note from the Japanese saying that they would pay $100 for everyone captured, dead or alive. Gladys sent a message back to the priest saying, "Tao Tu Pu Twai," (Christians never retreat)!

Instead, she would take the children to the government orphanage in Sian. They set out and walked for twelve days. Sometimes, people would give them a place to stay at night. Other times, they had no shelter and would have to sleep in the rugged mountains.

They arrived at Yellow River but all boat traffic had been stopped so there was no way to cross. They began to pray and sing. A Chinese officer rode up on horseback and got them a boat.

After crossing the river, Gladys became very ill with Typhus and was delirious for several days. However, all the children were safe and that was what mattered most.

Gladys returned to England for a badly needed operation and never went back to China but she preached Christ in England.

She had been a lone woman, facing all types of dangers. She had started a church in Sian and worked with lepers there. In 1970, she died, having had a life of victory, danger, suspense, and often, facing possible death. She had also been injured during the war with the Japanese. The world will never forget Gladys Aylward - they even made a film about her!

*"Go ye therefore, and teach all nations..."* (Matthew 28:19).

# Man of Faith

When Hudson Taylor was the ripe old age of four, he told his parents, "When I am a man, I mean to be a missionary and go to China." That is exactly what he did. Hudson Taylor was used more widely of God in China than any other missionary.

However, his bold statement about being a missionary and actually being one were different.

In his teen years, Hudson was very worldly and wild. His friends taught him how to scoff at important things and how to swear. He decided that he would get what he wanted from life, never thinking of anyone else.

One afternoon in 1849, bored and restless, Hudson went into his father's library to find something to read. He saw a Gospel tract titled, *"It Is Finished."* Curiously, he wondered "what was finished." What did that mean? He decided to find out and after reading the tract, he understood what Christ's death was about and why sins were paid for by His blood. His death finished the work of salvation.

At first, Hudson was full of excitement at accepting Christ but then he felt himself growing cold. He went away to be alone and it was then that he knew he had to go to China as a missionary. To prepare himself, he slept on a hard mattress, studied Greek, Latin, Hebrew, and Mandarin Chinese. He also threw himself into medicine so he could help the Chinese who had no doctor in the village.

On September 19, 1853, he sailed from Liverpool. He was finally going to be a missionary in China! However, all was not clear sailing. Two times, the ship, Dumfries, was within only a few feet of being wrecked. Once, it looked as though all hope was lost. They came within a few feet of New Guinea where cannibals were so sure the ship would crash that they had cooking fires flaming as they waited eagerly for their next meal.

Suddenly, a very strong current carried them toward the reefs. Surely, they were doomed? But Hudson and three other Christians prayed.

Hudson's favourite Bible verse came to mind and right away, he claimed it. "If you shall ask anything in my name, I will do it." (John 15:16) Immediately, the Lord sent a strong wind that sent them in the direction they wanted to go.

Hudson was only twenty-two years of age when he arrived in China and he was not ready for the civil war being waged in that country. He felt homesick, unhappy, and desolate. He was cold, had headaches, and eye problems but he was a man of faith. He decided to by boat along the Yangtze River with another man but the trip almost cost them their lives.

They visited fifty-eight villages from the boat. Only seven of the villages had ever seen a Protestant missionary. Hudson removed tumours, gave away books, and preached. However, the people seemed frightened and

58

angry and would sometimes throw mud and stones, fleeing from them. The only thing that saved them was Hudson's medical skills.

In 1856, Hudson married a fellow missionary named Maria. Both the Taylors were very sick but a child was born to them in 1859. One child died when very young and another died because it was born too early. Maria's lungs were so bad with tuberculosis that it took months for her to get her strength back after childbirth.

They went to a place called Ningpo where the heat was 103 degrees and where Grace, now six years old, died.

All sorts of dangers threatened them. Once their home was invaded and robbed. Maria was so sick she could not stand without help. Hudson admitted that he was so depressed at one point that he would have taken his life had it not been for Maria's love. Another child Noel was born in 1870 and lived for only thirteen days. Three days later, Maria also died.

Hudson married again. He wrote a friend saying, "We have 87 cents and all the promises of God." In June, they got a letter with $4,000 in it.

It seemed like everything was wrong. Four children dead, his first wife gone, and then the woman who cared for his other children in England died. Hudson and his second wife had to rush home to help. However on the ship, Hudson had a bad fall that left him paralyzed. He could only turn over in bed with the aid of a rope fixed above him. It seemed as though one thing after another was meant to discourage and defeat him.

At times, he would sing, "Jesus, I am resting, resting in the joy of what thou art." However, when he heard the awful news of hundreds of missionaries being killed, he said, "I cannot read. I cannot pray. I can scarcely think. However, I can trust."

Have you ever had times when it just seemed as though everything was going wrong? I have had times like that, which is why we have to keep our eyes fixed upon Jesus instead of what is happening around us. That is why Hudson Taylor was victorious!

*"Thou wilt keep him in perfect peace, whose mind is stayed on thee: because he trusteth in thee"* (Isaiah 26:3).

# Off to China

Isobel Kuhn went to Bible school for training at the Moody Bible Institute in the United States. Her dream was to go to China as a missionary.

Isobel would have to learn about the way they lived, which was far different from the way you and I live today. However, the real desire of her heart was to tell the people about Jesus. She wanted to tell them how He came to earth as a baby like you and me, how he grew to manhood, and how he went willingly to the cross where He was crucified for their sins and ours.

Isobel would have known that she would have to live in the same way that the Chinese did if she was going to live and work with them. Isobel longed to bring the Chinese to Christ.

While she was still in the United States Isobel met a man named John Kuhn who was also called to China as a missionary. They fell in love, got married, and together, they began their ministry.

They met a man called James Fraser and he deeply inspired them to go to the Lisu people to continue their ministry. After a while, John and Isobel moved into Lisu country and began a work together. They started several Bible schools and there, helped to strengthen the churches. John even became superintendent of the area after James Fraser died.

However, things started to go downhill for Isobel and John Kuhn. War broke out and communists began to take over China. What would the Kuhns do? They had a young son to think about and protect.

Thankfully, Isobel Kuhn was a strong and determined woman. She took her young son, Danny, and began a most dangerous trip across mountains that were more than 10,000 feet high. They were covered with snow. Bandits were known to roam the mountains, killing and stealing. Somehow, she fought her way over the Pienna Pass, which was an amazing 10,998 feet high. It would have been bitterly cold since this pass was a snowy, wind-swept mountain that she and her son would have to battle through. Isobel and Danny were willing to go through all this to escape the war and find freedom!

At last, she reached Upper Burma but her troubles were not yet over. Here, she was in a strange country where she could not speak the language. She did not even have any money and was still very far from home. The name of the place she was stranded in was Myitkyina, which translated into "The World's End." That was exactly what this place felt like to her.

She wrote, "I cannot tell you the dismay and alarm that filled me."

What could she do? Where could she turn? Isobel had to turn to the One who always hears our faintest cry and who listens to even our smallest and our greatest fears.

She remembered how when Jesus' disciples were frightened and scared Jesus would say to them, "Be not afraid." Jesus always came to their rescue.

Kneeling down in prayer, she confessed her fear and asked God to take it out of her heart. Picture her in your mind squaring her shoulders and saying, "I refuse to be afraid!"

Isobel was determined to find a way to get out of Asia, to get news to someone about where she was and that she needed help. She was also determined that from that day forward, she would "take it one day at a time." She would find food and money for her and her child.

Sometimes we cannot make things happen all at once the way we want them to. However, we are only supposed to take one day at a time. Jesus tells us not to worry about tomorrow. Looking beyond today can be dangerous and bewildering.

Isobel chose to trust God one day at a time for safety, food, and rescue. Eventually she made it back to the United States. She became a writer and wrote quite a few books where she told others about how God had looked after her.

*"Take therefore no thought for the morrow: for the morrow shall take thought for the things of itself" (Matthew 6:34).*

# The Lottie Moon Story

Many churches give an offering to mission work every Christmas in memory of Lottie Moon. Who was she? Lottie Moon was probably a bit of a rebel. She was called to serve God at a time when a woman was only really supposed to speak to a group of women. But Lottie was called to bring the Gospel to people who needed to hear of salvation.

She was born in Virginia, USA on December 12, 1840 and in the year 1859, Lottie gave her heart to Christ. It was not until 1873 though that she knew she wanted to be a missionary. She had gone to a meeting where a man preached about the fields being white for harvest, but the workers were few. Lottie was shocked to realize what that meant.

The fields were the world and people were waiting to hear the message of salvation, but ones who were willing to go and tell the good news about salvation through the blood of Jesus were very few.

She applied for service as a missionary with the Southern Baptist Mission Board, which then sent her to China. However, there was so much work to be done and so few missionaries that she pleaded for more missionaries to come and help.

She started the first Christmas offering in 1888. This money allowed three more missionaries to come to help with the work.

For fourteen years, Lottie worked for her Saviour in China before she took her first furlough to have a time of rest before returning to the work.

When Lottie went back to China some of her superiors were a bit concerned about her plans.

"It isn't fitting that a woman is going about building churches and 'preaching' in them!"

But Lottie was not one for wasting any time. So she did things that no other woman had ever dared to do. The mission board was horrified! They called her a "loose cannon (a rebel) prancing all over the mission field."

Another thing Lottie did that no woman had ever done was to wear Chinese clothing and live the way the Chinese lived. After all, what better way to gain their trust than to become one of them? Because of her work in China, that country and the church there, were wonderfully blessed by God.

When the great Chinese Famine came did Lottie become frightened and run away? No, she stayed and suffered hunger right along with the rest of them.

When she died in 1912, it was partly due to starvation. She had given away what little rice she had to those who were suffering so much.

And that is the story of Lottie Moon. A woman that the mission board had no idea what to do with, breaking all the rules. She rebelled by doing what God called her to do.

Through her words and work others heard about the everlasting life that is available through the blood of Jesus. Many of these people had never even heard of the name of Jesus and because Lottie Moon was obedient these people were given the opportunity to hear God's word and accept salvation.

Lottie Moon, was a single woman and because of what she did she changed the way women were treated even to this very day. She knew what God had called her to do and that she had to obey. So that is what she did.

*"We ought to obey God rather than men"* *(Acts 5:29).*

# Mom Keymer

It was a bitterly cold night and Mom Keymer was slipping on a warm flannel nightgown.

Mom Keymer was the pianist in a little Christian church in Tucson, Arizona. She must have had a first name, as most everyone does but if she did, no one knew it. She was "Mom Keymer", a sweet, spiritual, white-haired woman.

Far on the other side of the world in the high rugged mountains of Tibet, a missionary and his wife, Mr. and Mrs. Schmidt, had been visiting a tiny village tucked away, hidden from the world. Sometimes, they drove the rough trails from one home to another, trying to reach the people with the message of God's grace.

Tibet was a land of mystery and wonder. Men farmed the hillsides and tended their herds of yak, which provided them with milk, curds, and butter.

The home the missionaries were leaving was a blockhouse made of wood and stone. The lower floor was where the animals bedded down at night. The people were friendly and seemed eager to know more about the Gospel. Now, they solemnly shook hands. While the missionaries were shivering in the cold, the

Tibetan family was cosy in their sheepskin outerwear, the furry side turned toward their bodies.

The missionaries did not want to drive through the wooded mountains after dark because of the danger of bandits. Therefore, they started out early down the steep, winding mountains.

Mr. Schmidt pressed the brake when he came to a hairpin curve but the brakes did not work! Repeatedly, he tried to slow the vehicle but it was hurling out of control down the winding road. Sweating, his knuckles white on the steering wheel, he cried, "Dear God in heaven, have mercy. Protect us!"

Mrs. Schmidt was quoting scripture while she clung to the edges of her seat. *"Thou shalt not be afraid for the terror by night" (Psalm 91:5).*

They screeched around the sharp curves. Sometimes, they felt the rear end of the vehicle swing out into the air before it found the ground again.

"God, please have someone pray for us!" pleaded Mrs. Schmidt.

A world away, Mom Keymer was suddenly awakened. An inner voice said, "Pray for the Schmidts."

"What?" she whispered. "I don't know anyone named Schmidt."

But the inner voice persisted, "Pray for the Schmidts." Throwing back the covers, Mom Keymer placed her bony knees on the cold floor and prayed fervently for the name that had been given to her.

Mr. Schmidt was wrestling with the steering wheel but it was a losing battle. Then suddenly and miraculously, they reached the bottom of the mountains safely.

Mr. Schmidt bowed his head on the steering wheel. "God, thank you!"

"Someone's been praying," whispered his wife.

Someone was and it was Mom Keymer. She told the people in church on Sunday about the strange experience. But it wasn't until the next month when the missionary magazine came out that her friends realised what had happened. There in print was the story of some missionaries named Schmidt and their narrow escape from death as they came plummeting out of control down the mountains in Tibet.

Now do you see how very important it is to obey the voice of God when He speaks to our hearts, even when we do not understand?

*"Be anxious for nothing; but in every thing, by prayer and supplication with thanksgiving, let your requests be known unto God. And the peace of God, which passeth all understanding, shall keep your hearts and minds through Christ Jesus" (Philippians 4:6-7).*

# Mother of the Nile

Born on September 27, 1887, Lillian Trasher grew up in Brunswick, Georgia. One day, while still a young girl she knelt by a fallen log all alone in the woods. "Lord," she prayed, "if ever I can do anything for you, just let me know and I'll do it."

God had a plan and years later, a woman named Miss Perry asked Lillian to work for her at an orphanage. This led to her going to Elhanah Training Institute where she learned how to care for babies, cook, and sew. Large numbers of small children came into her care and it was at this institute she learned to trust God for the needs of life. All this time God was answering her childhood prayer but she did not know it.

She had no money and humbled herself to wear an old pair of men's shoes. She also met a wonderful young man and in ten days, they planned to marry.

Lillian was sensing a call to the mission field but with her wedding only ten days away, it seemed impossible, that is until she went with Miss Perry to hear a missionary from India. His sermon touched her so deeply that she cried all the way home.

Miss Perry asked her what was wrong and Lillian told her that God had just called her to

Africa and that she was to be married in ten days. It was all so impossible.

Knowing that obeying God was more important than getting married, she gathered her few belongings and prepared to leave for the mission field. She believed God would provide a way to Africa – and He did. Both Lillian and her sister, Jenny, were on their way to Africa just a short time later. However, Lillian needed a promise from God. She opened her Bible and read these words, *"I have seen the affliction of my people, which is in Egypt and I have heard their groaning and am come down to deliver them. And now come, I will send thee to Egypt."* To Egypt it was!

Travelling down river by boat Egypt seemed to Lillian to be the most beautiful place in the world. A little while later, though, she saw the dirty, ragged, homeless children, children that nobody wanted.

One night, a man knocked at their door and asked the sisters to come and pray for his sick wife. They were horrified to enter the home and see a small baby sucking stringy green milk from a tin can. The smell told them that she had probably never been bathed. Before the mother died, she gave the baby to Lillian and Jenny but the baby girl never stopped crying. The other missionaries demanded they take her back from where she came. Lillian was horrified. She was supposed to obey those who were in charge over her but she could not.

Lillian decided that she would have to take the baby back but that she would go with her to stay.

"What?" her superior demanded. "A single woman living with Arabs? Don't be so foolish,

Lillian. You'll starve to death, maybe even be killed."

Lillian was a large woman with brown hair and a voice like thunder, "My mind is made up. God will take care of us."

After renting a tiny house and some furniture, she had no money left. The mission board gave her nothing and with her sister back in the States, she had to beg. She got just enough money for a day's food - thirty-five cents worth. People still gave her their babies though. Lillian took them and looked after them as much as she could.

However sometimes she had terrible problems. Once she could not get back to the children and had to spend a night in a jail cell with a donkey. However, Lillian felt that if a donkey was good enough for Jesus, it was good enough for her.

Eventually people began to send her barrels of clothing and sometimes money. Her Egyptian neighbours also helped. She told them of God's power to save them from sin.

When the babies kept coming Lillian told the Lord she would care for them but that He must give her money. Lord MacLay from Scotland came to her orphanage and gave her $100. Later, convicted that he had not given enough, he gave $5,000. Then he gave $20,000!

Lillian had given up marriage because she loved Jesus the most. Often she never knew where the next meal would come from. However, Lillian Trasher was happy and never looked back on what she could have had. Today, years after her death, her orphanage is still one of the largest in the world.

*"And every one that hath forsaken houses, or brethren, or sisters, or father, or mother, or wife, or children, or lands, for my name's sake, shall receive an hundredfold, and shall inherit everlasting life"* (Matthew 19:29).

Cedar Valley Christian School
3636 Cottage Grove Ave SE
Cedar Rapids, IA  52403

# Captured

Tak'ke was sitting outside his thatch and bamboo home under the stars. His parents had named him Tak'ke because it meant "lizard". With such an ugly name, they were sure the evil spirits would leave him alone.

Missionaries had come to his village not long ago and built a small church. Tak'ke had given his heart to Jesus, so he should be a very happy boy but he did not feel happy at all. He had just come from the church and saw men sitting around a fire drinking, with his father being one of them. Tak'ke knelt and prayed that tonight his father would not get drunk again. If only he knew Jesus and how Jesus could change his life. To make things worse, Tak'ke hated the gongs that called forth evil spirits!

On a pole close by was the head of a buffalo that had been sacrificed so they would have a good rice crop. However, the sacrifice had done no good, for while the men were clearing a field, a deer had barked nearby. That was a bad sign so the men had to go somewhere else and begin clearing another field.

Another bad thing was that the Communists were coming closer every day. Sometimes, they would catch a Vietnamese and that person would never be seen again. The Communists would take him away and force him to do very hard work.

Finally, Tak'ke went to sleep on his straw mat but he was up again at dawn. He took his crossbow, hoping to kill a deer so his family would have meat. Stopping at the little bamboo church the missionaries had built, he knelt to pray. "Lord, I put myself in Your hands today. Keep me true to You forever."

Tak'ke was at home in the jungle, but when he saw the pugmarks of a tiger, a flash of terror washed over him. There was great superstition among his people that if you stepped into the footprints of a tiger, terrible danger would come to you.

Feeling daring, he prayed, "Lord Jesus, now that I know You, I no longer believe that superstition."

He clenched his teeth and stepped into the tiger's prints. He must be free from the old superstitions!

He had walked about three miles when suddenly three men leaped from the shadows. With them were two tribesmen - Communists! They were wicked men who burned down churches, killed missionaries, and tried to take over the country.

In confusion, Tak'ke dropped his crossbow and turned to flee, but the men leaped upon him and captured him.

A huge bag of rice lay on the ground. One of the men pointed to it and said, "Come. We need you to carry the rice."

It was impossible, the rice was too heavy and each time they placed it on his shoulders, he promptly fell down.

Satan whispered into Tak'ke's heart, "See, you angered the evil spirits by stepping onto the tiger's prints."

"Pick up the rice!" one of the men snarled.

A Scripture verse the missionaries had taught him was, *"... greater is he that is in you, than he that is in the world" (1 John 4:4).*

One of the men struck Tak'ke in the face. "Pick it up! You stupid boy, carry the rice or else!"

"It is too heavy for him," another man protested as they placed the rice on his shoulders once more. Tak'ke only fell down again. He felt them kicking him and he curled up in a knot. "Jesus, the missionaries said if I was in trouble and called on You..."

One of the men picked up the rice. "Go on home, little girl! We'll find someone bigger and stronger to work for us."

Wasting no time, Tak'ke raced back down the narrow jungle path to his village. Jesus had answered just as the missionaries said He would. Once he was safe, Tak'ke knelt to thank God. He knew he was kneeling beside some bamboo where his people believed evil spirits lived, but he was not afraid. He knew for sure now that his God was more powerful than any evil spirit.

*"And call upon me in the day of trouble; I will deliver thee, and thou shalt glorify me" (Psalm 50:15).*

# Story of the Pygmies

Bob Pruett and Ernie Rebb were making a second trip into the bush country of the Philippine Islands. They wanted to see how the black Pygmies were getting along in their new faith in Christ. The faith of the two men was high and their steps light. It was a high and holy calling to teach new Christians how to live for Christ.

By the end of the first day however, the heat and the insects began troubling them. It seemed as though hours were spent wringing water from their sweatbands and swatting at the army of insects attacking them. Sun helmets did little to keep the sizzling heat from beating down on their heads.

Depression set in and their steps lagged. They were weary yet tried to hold back their feelings. They had two more days, hopeless days, to go before reaching the tribe of the black Pygmies.

It was their second day out before either of the missionaries confessed their own feelings.

Sweaty, dirty, and tired, Ernie sank down on a fallen tree and dropped his head to his chest. With one hand, he swatted at insects and with the other hand, wiped the sweat from his face.

"Sometimes, Bob, I wonder why we're doing this," Ernie confided.

Bob sighed deeply. "You too?"

"I hate to admit it, but this entire trip seems so useless," Ernie brooded. "We brought these people the message of salvation and then we had to leave them. The only teaching they've had since then is when a native pastor visits them maybe once every two months. I don't know if we can even expect them to live their lives for Christ."

Bob took off his sun helmet and ran his fingers through his damp hair. "I'm afraid you're right, Ernie, but look, we're more than halfway there now. Let's pay them a quick visit. Maybe we can at least tell them about Jesus' love one more time. After that, well, we'll have to leave them on their own again."

"Poor little tribe," Ernie breathed sadly. "What can God expect of them anyway?"

They walked on slowly. The heat and constant buzzing of insects was maddening. Everything in the two men wanted to call it quits, to turn their backs and try to put the Pygmy tribe out of their minds forever.

They felt that it just was not worth it, trying once more to touch a small tribe that the world did not even know existed! A lot of people thought that the Pygmy tribe was just made up of small black people with bones in their noses and rings in their ears! "They're uncivilised, they know nothing. It's a waste of time teaching them anything," some people argued.

By the end of the third day, the missionaries were dragging one foot after the other. All hope of ever teaching the Pygmies about spiritual things was almost gone. Defeat nagged at them with each step.

It was just becoming dark and Bob and his companion were pulling their weary bodies up the last long hill. On the other side of that hill was where the tribe of Pygmies lived. The men almost dreaded their meeting with them.

Just before reaching the top of the hill, the men fell to the ground to rest for a minute. It was dark now and a little breeze was blowing. Ernie removed his helmet and laid his tired head in his arms. A few seconds later, he twisted his head and listened. "Bob, do you hear something?"

Bob stopped and listened too. "I thought I did."

The men sat up, listening intently. Slowly, their faces turned to frowns of bewilderment.

"Ernie, I hear singing."

Ernie shook his head, "It can't be."

Bob took a few steps further and stood there speechless. Below him was a huge bonfire. Around the fire was the Pygmy tribe, with bones in their noses and rings in their ears. Their faces glowed with happiness in the flickering firelight. Their heads were bowed in prayer and then they were singing again.

Ernie joined Bob and they listened in disbelief as the Pygmies joyfully sang a hymn to Jesus.

Faces aglow, the tribe stood around the fire sharing bits of food and drinking sips of juice from a single cup.

"They're celebrating the death and resurrection of Christ," Ernie whispered.

Humbled and ashamed, the two men walked down the hill to join the Pygmies in their devotion to Christ. They ate the bits of coarse bread, the symbol of Christ's body and they sipped the juice, the symbol of His blood.

Sometimes, we fail to understand that when Jesus buys us with His own blood, He keeps us forever.

*"Being confident of this very thing, that he which hath begun a good work in you will perform it until the day of Jesus Christ. (Philippians 1:6).*

# Tell Me His Name Again

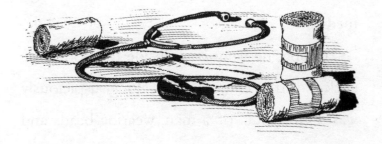

Jim Archer stood on the hill overlooking the wild African country. He was there at last and the clinic he had dreamed of, poor though it was, was slowly drawing the people in for treatment. The natives had never heard of Christ's love and had never known that He had died for their sins. They had never heard the name of Jesus.

Jim smiled a lopsided smile. He was a medical missionary at last! His voice was not loud for preaching but he prayed that God could use him to reach the people one at a time through medicine.

Turning, he went back inside the poor little stick and straw clinic. Trailing along suspiciously was a great hulk of a man, wearing beads and feathers. A string of animal teeth was around his neck. A running, open sore caused him enough pain to overcome his fear and suspicion of the white man – he must have treatment! He was an important man, the village witch doctor.

Smiling, Jim and his wife Elizabeth welcomed him into the clinic. Gently, Jim examined the terrible sore on the witch doctor's leg and as he worked, he began speaking to the witch doctor about salvation.

The man showed no emotion at all until, that is, Jim spoke the name of Jesus. There was a swift change on the witch doctor's face. He grew still and his face showed both anger and horror. His leg, only half wrapped, did not stop him from leaping to his feet. Limping badly, he raced down the slope and disappeared into the wild, brushy land.

Screams of terror and rage flew behind him. "Don't say that name! Don't ever say that name again!"

Jim and his wife stared after the man in disbelief.

"No missionary has ever been here before. There is no way that witch doctor could have known the name of Jesus."

Elizabeth whispered, "But Jim, remember that he serves evil spirits. All evil spirits know the name of Jesus and they can't bear to hear it."

Jim sighed. "Of course. That's exactly what drove that man away."

During the following days, Jim did not meet the witch doctor again but he knew he would never forget him. The agony the witch doctor must have suffered caused Jim sleepless nights.

The witch doctor knew he did not have long to live unless something was done. Something else was troubling him too. He forced himself to think the word. Say it aloud – "Jesus!"

Hobbling painfully up the slope toward the clinic with a crude crutch under one arm, the witch doctor clenched his teeth and waited politely until he was invited inside. Sitting down on a stool, he stretched out his leg. Jim unwound the soaked bandages and was horrified by the infection that was poisoning the witch doctor's life. If he had not come back when he did, Jim would have had to amputate the leg.

As Jim worked and tenderly treated the infected leg, he once again began to tell the witch doctor about a "Heavenly Chief" who had died to forgive his sins. However, Jim was careful not to mention the name of Jesus.

The witch doctor waited silently. A look of wistfulness filled his ebony face. "The name," he whispered at last, "please tell me His name again."

Jim thought the witch doctor might actually break down and cry. "I have never heard of the Jesus tribe but the evil spirits knew His name. Please sir, I want to join this Jesus tribe."

Jim talked about Jesus well after he finished dressing the wound. He watched as Satan released his hold of the witch doctor.

With his life changed, the village people wanted to know what had happened to their witch doctor. People accepted Christ and idols and other things used in the worship of the evil spirits were burned. These items included animal teeth, beads, anything that the natives felt held great power. Jim was one man, yet God used him to turn an entire village to faith in Christ.

You may think you are nothing and that God cannot work great things through you but you are wrong.

When we allow the Holy Spirit to guide our lives, He can do wonderful things through us. Of course, it does not have to be on the mission field. He can use you right where you are!

Remember, it was only one man, Elijah, whom God used to turn the hearts of a nation back to God. Elijah made a challenge – the God that sent fire to burn up the animal sacrifice would be the true God. The fire fell on Elijah's sacrifice.

*"And when all the people saw it, they fell on their faces: and they said, The LORD, he is the God; the LORD, he is the God!" (1 Kings 18:39).*

# The God of Daniel is Here

Justin Buckamye was a native pastor in a wild part of the African jungle. He was almost too excited to sleep for tomorrow was Easter, and a great celebration had been planned. The jungle surrounding his village would come alive with people gathering for a feast. They would carry bundles of food on their heads and wear smiles on their faces. After the feast, they would head to the native church made of sticks and thatch for a preaching service. Oh yes, it was going to be a wonderful day!

By 10:00 the next morning, joyful singing could be heard as the natives came swarming along the jungle paths to the village. The jungle was not dark and gloomy now but alive with colour. Reds, blues, greens, and yellows – for these people loved bright turbans and skirts.

Tables set up under the huge banyan trees. Large tree trunks were used as tables and loaded with wild, sweet potatoes, a roasted goat, and fresh fruit from the jungle.

The morning was filled with visiting, laughter, singing, and feasting. Then, it was time for the preaching.

Looking out over the huge crowd, Rev. Buckamye sighed and wondered what to do. So many people could not begin to crowd into the small church.

Standing just outside the church door on the top step, he shouted, "We'll need to have the service outdoors because there just isn't enough room inside."

Then, a sudden stir occurred among the people, as a man came running from the jungle screaming in terror and waving his arms. "A lion," he cried. "A man-eating lion is headed this way. It has already killed three goats, a woman, and her two children!"

People were stunned and terrified. How could such a beautiful, sunny day turn into such disaster, and there were so many people, where could they go? Where could they hide?

Huddled together in terror, women began crying, as the children clung to them in fear. The men had no idea what to do. Some of them had swords or spears but the people were crammed too tightly together to take action. Besides, no one knew for sure where the lion was.

Then, a mighty roar pierced the air, as a large, tawny beast came lumbering out from the jungle. Its fangs were white and deadly, dripping saliva as it looked for its next meal.

For a moment, it seemed that Justin Buckamye could not move or think what to do. Then, he remembered Daniel in the lion's den. God had shut the lion's mouth to protect his servant from harm. Well, God's power was just the same today and He had promised His children that same power. Suddenly, with a shout, Justin leaped through the air and dashed through the dense crowd. Pointing a finger at the snarling lion, he shouted, "People, fear not. The God of Daniel is with us!"

114

It was a warm, sunny day. There was not a cloud in the sky – no thunder and no rain, yet suddenly, a bolt of lightening shot from the heavens and the lion dropped to the earth, dead!

Maybe you and I will never experience anything like that but it is still true that God has given us His power. He never intended for us to be weak or frightened of any enemy.

*"Behold, I give unto you power to tread on serpents and scorpions, (evil forces) and over all the power of the enemy: and nothing shall by any means hurt you" (Luke 10:19).*

# Trapped in Mau Mau Land

The Mau Mau was the most feared tribe in Africa. To be found in their territory could mean death! Rev. and Mrs. Jackson had been ministering in faraway villages for years. They knew they must drive through the dreaded Mau Mau country on their way home so they started for the mission station while it was still light outside. To their horror, while it was becoming dark their van broke down.

Unable to repair the vehicle in the dark, the Jacksons prayed, placing themselves in the hands of their Heavenly Father.

Thrilled that God had kept them safe through the night, in the morning, Rev. Jackson fixed the vehicle. Driving into a village, they found a small café where they could eat breakfast. The owner eyed them suspiciously before asking them a strange question.

"Where are the others?" he demanded suspiciously.

"Others?" Rev. Jackson echoed.

"The other men," the café owner insisted.

The Jacksons looked puzzled. "But we are alone."

"This morning," the man began, "some Mau Mau came in for something to eat. They said they found your vehicle broken down with you sleeping inside. They decided to rob and kill you but as they crept toward your vehicle in the dark, they saw sixteen strong men surrounding you. They knew they could never overtake so many so they turned around, running in fear."

"But," Rev. Jackson frowned, "there were no men."

"Sixteen," the man repeated firmly. "Mau Mau would not lie about something like that."

Alone, the Jacksons puzzled over this mystery for days.

"Maybe God sent angels to protect us," Mrs. Jackson suggested.

"Maybe," Rev. Jackson murmured. "I guess we'll never know."

Some months later, they returned home to the United States for a time of rest and preaching in various churches. After a service one particular night, a friend approached them with the question, "Tell me – was there ever a time when you were in great danger in Africa?"

The Jacksons shared the strange story of their survival in the terrible Mau Mau country. Their friend said, "At that very time, God gave me great heaviness in my heart for you. I felt you needed urgent prayer so I gathered fifteen other men and we went to the church where we prayed until we believed that you were safe."

The Jacksons were shocked. Somehow, God had made it appear to the Mau Mau, as if the sixteen friends had actually been standing, encircling the vehicle to protect the two missionaries.

The Jacksons' friend was beaming when he heard this. "I don't know how God did it, but that's exactly what happened."

So you see, God is a God of mystery. He is also a God of miracles. He is always there to care for us and watch over us.

*"But as it is written, Eye hath not seen, nor ear heard, neither have entered into the heart of man, the things which God hath prepared for them that love him" (1Corinthians 2:9).*

# Voodoo Village

The jungle was alive with the sound of clicking, buzzing, roaring, and chattering of monkeys.

When the Reverend Tom Arnold and his companion, Jim Evers, spoke to one another, they had to speak loudly in order to be heard.

The noise was so loud, you could hardly hear yourself think! Let alone hold a conversation with anyone.

A chill passed over Jim though the air was hot and moist. "Well, old friend, we've put our lives in God's hands. We may not come out of this village alive, you know."

Tom took a deep breath. "That is, if what all the other natives say about this village is true."

"I hate voodoo," Jim said fiercely. "Think of it. Using charms to try to put spells and curses on other people. It's devil worship for sure!"

Just then there was a sudden hush in the jungle. The monkeys stopped howling and the wild chirping softened. What was going on? Then, two young native boys appeared on the narrow trail ahead of them.

They too stopped, stunned at the sight of the two white men. At first, they looked confused, a little fearful and then, broad smiles of joy lit up their faces.

"You have come to us at last. Come with us. Let us take you to our village."

Jim flashed a look of bewilderment at Tom. Was the village about to have them for supper? Had white men been to the village before?

The boys grasped their hands and dragged them along quickly. The smell of cooking fires met them. People were chattering as they appeared. Soon there were shouts of joy.

The Chief appeared from his hut and bowed low before the men. "You have come at last!" The string of tiger teeth rattled around his neck. "We have waited so long. Please, now you are here – teach us about the Jesus tribe."

What in the world was going on? Why, this was no voodoo village. These people were not cannibals.

"I don't understand," Jim managed through dry lips. "How could you know we were coming?"

The Chief's black face was radiant. "Come. I show you." He led the men to a tiny thatch and bamboo hut. Slowly, he opened the door and showed them what was inside. The white men staggered with disbelief. The only things in the hut were a table and upon the table, a Bible.

Tom Arnold blinked. "A Bible, but where did it come from?"

The Chief said soberly, "Once, a long time ago, a runner from the coast came and brought Bibles with him. He was very sick and could not stay. He tried to reach as many villages as possible before he died. He said to gather my people around the Bible every day and pray that God, the real God would send a white man to come and teach us how to join the Jesus tribe."

The missionaries were both fighting back tears.

The Bible had no dust on it. The bamboo table looked polished. The missionaries could see in their minds the entire village gathering around that Bible every day, praying that an unknown God would send a white man to teach them what was in that book, someone to help them understand the love of Jesus.

Tom Arnold spoke to the Chief in a broken voice, "Tell me, how long have you been praying for the white man to come?"

The Chief's dark, leathery face was very sober. "Twenty summers."

The missionaries almost choked. "Twenty… but that would mean twenty years."

The Chief nodded. "For twenty summers we have prayed for a white man to come and tell us how to join the Jesus tribe."

With a humble heart, Tom preached to the village that night and every single person old enough to understand gave their heart to Jesus Christ.

What do you do? Perhaps you pray about something once, twice, maybe a dozen times? If God does not answer, do you give up? Think of how these natives must have longed to hear about Jesus Christ. They wanted it so badly that they prayed for twenty, long years!

Perhaps God wanted to answer their prayer long before. Perhaps he called some man or woman to go to preach to these people? Perhaps that man or woman refused? We should be careful to listen to God's call and to obey him when he asks us to serve him. In God's word it says that we should love God with all our hearts, strength and mind and our neighbour as ourselves.

Perhaps you will be part of someone's answer to prayer. Perhaps today someone is asking God for a preacher or teacher. If today or in the future God calls you to serve him, obey him with all your heart. If you are praying to God and have been praying for ever such a long time ... keep praying ... keep praying ... keep praying!

*"And I say unto you, Ask, and it shall be given you; seek, and you shall find; knock, and it shall be opened unto you" (Luke 11:9).*

# White Queen of Calabar

White Queen of Calabar - that is what the natives
called Mary Slessor, a Scottish missionary. She
ministered on the West Coast of Africa and it
was said that she could even conquer cannibals.
In a way, she really was a queen, but she was
a queen who won people by love and kindness.
Yet, as we shall soon see, she was a queen who
could be tough and stand up to the vicious Chief

who would have done terrible things to people when his son died.

Like Paul the Apostle, she knew hunger, thirst, and faced danger and death hundreds of times. She rescued twin babies that were thrown into the forest and left to die of starvation or to be eaten by wild animals. She saw twenty-five heads cut off because a Chief died. Another time, a Chief died and sixty people were killed and eaten. Mary Slessor lived among killers and cannibals and came back to Scotland with four of the babies that she had rescued from certain death.

Even when she was young, Mary had a desire to go to Calabar. She worked hard in her own church, but her heart was in Africa. Finally, she offered her services to the Foreign Mission

Board, had some special training in Edinburgh and on August 5, 1876 left Liverpool on a steamer bound for Calabar in Africa.

However, Calabar was no picnic. Danger was found everywhere. Enormous alligators lay on muddy river banks in the sun. They hid in the water, ready to devour anything that came their way. One time, she was in a canoe with some children when a hippopotamus attacked them. Mary picked up a cooking pot, threw it at the hippo's open jaws, and it soon ran away. Mary's actions had saved her and her children from drowning.

Natives were tested in terrible ways to see if they were guilty of some crime. One way was to make them drink poison. If they died, which of course they did, that proved they were guilty. If they did not die, they were innocent. Another way was to make a suspected criminal dip his hand into boiling oil. If his hand was not hurt, he was innocent, but if his hand was burned, then he was guilty.

It was terrible for Mary to see these brutal practices. She hated to see slaves put into pens, to wait for the ships to arrive to take them away. More hideous than anything, though, was to see a Chief's wife either buried alive or strangled when her husband died.

The natives had their own set of laws and all of them were too terrible to see or believe. Mary became very depressed and asked the Lord what she should do, for the work was too hard for her. Only the Lord could give her the strength and wisdom to live among cannibals.

The natives called her "Ma", and one day someone screamed, "Run, Ma, run!" She hurried into the forest, where she found the son of the Chief lying under a fallen tree. For two weeks, she did everything she knew to save him, but he finally died.

The Chief, Edem, was heartbroken and blamed the death of his son on witchcraft. The witch doctor came and said the boy's death could be blamed on a certain village. Soldiers were sent to the village and brought back a dozen men and women in chains.

Mary dressed Edem's son for the funeral, putting him in the finest clothes she could find. She made everything look really grand - hoping that perhaps this might make the chief happier and possibly save lives. Meanwhile, the savages drank liquor constantly. One barrel of rum would be emptied and another would be opened. The people behaved as if they had been driven mad. When Mary could not bear to see the terrified, half-starved prisoners writhing in torment, she took charge. Relying on the help of the Holy Spirit, she confronted the Chief, pleading with him not to put the prisoners to the poison test.

They argued for a long time but finally, the Chief let the prisoners go. This was unheard of. It was a miracle. The custom for those tribes was that when someone died a violent death as the Chief's son had, the grave would be covered with human blood. However, instead, this time a cow was killed instead of a human. This had never happened before.

It is amazing to think of Mary Slessor, a single woman living alone in a savage tribe who thought nothing of cutting off people's heads or eating them. How did she have such courage? It was only by the grace of God.

She learned to speak their language as well as they did and faithfully preached the word of God to the savages. They were cruel and sinful but even so, Mary spoke to them of the love of Jesus and told them they could have eternal life through His blood.

She had lived in a mud hut, ate what they ate, drank muddy water, and slept on the ground. All to win the lost natives to Jesus Christ!

*"I am the resurrection, and the life: he that believeth in me, though he were dead, yet shall he live" (John 11:25).*

# The Pathfinder

He was born in a village in Scotland in 1813. His name is known around the world, is still spoken about in classrooms, and is written in history books. His name is David Livingstone.

David went to school in the village until he was ten and then quit school to go to work in a cotton mill. I wonder if any of you can even imagine quitting school at age ten and working in a mill! However, in spite of the hard work, David was determined that one day he would go back to school!

In fact as soon as he was able to leave the cotton mill, David went to college. There he studied Greek, medicine, and the Bible. Then when he was still a very young man, he sailed from England in December 1840. His goal was to travel through Africa. To him, it was like an itch he could not scratch, this desire was so great.

For two years, David roamed the remote wilderness of Africa. He ventured into places no white man had never set foot. Some people called him "The Pathfinder" because he made paths for others to follow.

Once he was attacked by a lion. His left arm was crushed yet he managed to shoot the lion. However, it was too late to save his arm.

David learned the languages of the natives and treated them as he would have treated anyone else. He loved the Africans and was shocked at the way men from other countries treated them. The Livingstone writings were responsible for showing the world the evils of slave trading. In his writings, he called it the "open sore of Africa."

For thirty years, he was missionary, doctor, and explorer. David was a gentle man who understood the natives' terror of the white man. After all, many white men were slave traders. However, Livingstone brought them hope and healing instead.

Some of you may have heard of Victoria Falls. David Livingstone was the first white man to set eyes on it. He named it Victoria after the queen of his native land. Today, this is still one of the world's greatest wonders.

David was loved and welcomed by the natives, but the slave traders hated him. Through his writings, he earned enough money to help fight the slave trade, explore the far reaches of Africa, and practice medicine with the native tribes.

Suddenly, Livingstone disappeared. For years, he seemed to have vanished from the face of the earth. Had he died? Was he lost? The New York Herald wanted to know so they sent another explorer, Henry M. Stanley, to search for him. It took a long time, but Stanley finally found Livingstone in November 1871 in a small town on a lake called Tanganyika. Recognizing David at once, he greeted David Livingstone with the famous words, "Dr. Livingstone, I presume?"

David never did find the Nile, but his explorations are a part of history. His determination never faltered. He was a gentle

Scottish missionary, doctor, and much, much more.

In 1865 at the age of 62, David made his last journey, even though it was not long. David had lost his medical supplies, animals, and even those who worked with him. Now, almost alone in a foreign land, everything was gone. David struggled ahead anyway since he never quit!

At one village, he saw slave traders killing the natives. He wrote home telling of the horror he had seen and the British government tried to stop it although they never completely succeeded.

On April 30, 1872, Henry Stanley brought the supplies David needed but instead of helping, he found David's body kneeling by his bed. He had died while praying, being identified by his useless left arm. What a story and adventure. God had called David Livingstone and he had answered the call to the end. The Bible says, *"Faithful is he that calleth you, who also will do it"* *(1 Thessalonians 5:24).*

If God calls you to do something, whether something big or small, He will always make sure that you have what you need to fulfil that call.

# The Martyr

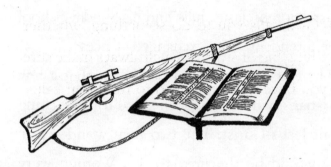

At the end of a little, dusty road in Central America sat a poor mud church. The pastor, Julio Martinez, stood tall and confident, preaching to his people. However, things were uneasy in his country and Christianity was not welcomed.

A sound came from down the street, perhaps somewhere near the river. It was the thud of leather boots and rifles, as they swished against uniforms.

People grew tense. Julio knew the soldiers were coming to the church. A frown creased his forehead but he went right on preaching the death and resurrection of Jesus. Julio and his Sunday School Superintendent, Juan, exchanged glances.

The outside world did not know that a few Christians had already been killed for preaching about Jesus Christ. The two men wondered if they would be the next to die. Women were crying, children were clinging to their mothers, and the men did not move.

The soldiers faces filled with anger as they stormed the church. Julio knew that these soldiers wanted to stop the voice of the Gospel in this village.

Both Julio and Juan calmly stepped back. "What do you want here?" Julio asked.

Two soldiers came to the pulpit, grabbing Julio by the shoulders and dragging him from the church. An angry command was given by a superior officer.

Behind Julio, Juan was also dragged from the church and both men were prodded with automatic weapons, moving them toward the river. They were forced to stand with their backs against a railing. The soldiers cursed with hatred spilling from their black eyes.

"Hands in the air," the superior officer screamed at Julio. He obeyed as Juan watched helplessly.

There were seven soldiers, all with weapons pointing directly at Julio. They knew their orders would soon be coming.

"Are you willing to deny this God you follow and stop preaching this foolishness?"

Julio felt a great calm come over him as he answered, "Never."

"Don't you realize that you will be shot? I can spare your life if you promise to give up this Gospel you preach."

Julio smiled, "Jesus Christ gave His life and shed His blood. I can never give Him up!"

The officer's face turned bright red. Turning to the seven soldiers, he screamed, "FIRE!" Seven loud shots rang out and Julio tumbled into the river.

Juan was forced against the railing next.

"You worked with that preacher," accused the officer. "What will you do? Deny this Christ and live, follow Him and die."

Juan felt pale and was trembling. He wanted to be calm. "I will never deny my Lord," he said. "You will have to shoot me, as you shot my friend."

"You are a fool," the man snarled.

"But I would like to pray before I die," Juan declared.

The officer crossed his arms and waited with disgust while Juan prayed, "Father, these men do not understand what they are doing. Please don't punish them. Now I ask you to receive my spirit."

As in a dream, Juan heard the guns click and then the order to fire.

Juan waited but did not hear anything. Every eye turned to one young soldier who had laid his rifle down. He turned on his heels and walked off the bridge. For a long time, the other soldiers stared after him. What had just happened? Uncertainty showed on their faces and some bit their lips.

Then, one by one, the other six soldiers stooped, laid down their weapons, and walked away. The superior officer cursed and hopped around in fury, yet he did not want to be the only one to fire. Juan was safe.

Weeks went by and then Juan became the new pastor. The church was packed. Sitting up front were seven men with shining faces. They had been the seven soldiers who had thrown down their guns, walking off the bridge that day. Touched by what Julio and Juan had said, these men had given their hearts to Jesus. Now, they were doing everything they could to win others to Christ.

We don't know who will be touched by our faithful testimony for Christ but as the Bible says, *"Therefore if any man be in Christ, he is a new creature: old things are passed away; behold, all things are become new" (2 Corinthians 5:17).*

# The Meaning of Grace

Everyone talks about the grace of God, but what does the word "grace" mean? It means getting something you do not deserve and cannot earn – like our salvation.

Now then, let us play a guessing game. I will give you some clues and you see if you can name this man before I write about him.

He was born in London in 1725, his mother died when he was seven, and at the age of eleven, he went to sea with his father. He had only two years of schooling.

He had no use for God and would curse and mock Him. Other sailors feared that he would go to hell. He got into the slave business to make money and finally had his own slave ship. Only when his ship was about to sink during a very bad storm did this man cry out to God.

He became a Christian and wrote many hymns. One is so famous that you have probably sung it time after time in your own church. Can you guess who he is?

With only two years of school, John Newton went to sea with his father. He made six voyages before his father retired. When he was nineteen, he was forced to serve his country on a Man-of-War ship named H.M.S. Harwich. However, the ship was an awful place to live. The food was wormy, rats were everywhere, and there was always stinking water sloshing under the hammocks in the Seamans' quarters.

It was so bad that John jumped ship. Things were even worse when he was recaptured and flogged in front of all the sailors. His back was cut to ribbons from the whip and he lay in his hammock groaning in misery. After that, his rank was cut from mid-ship man to common seaman.

John Newton hated God. He would go into a wicked dance on ship, laughing, cursing, and mocking God until he made the other sailors fear that God would punish them all. John had no such fear of God at all.

Unable to bear the awful conditions on the Man-of-War, he asked to be transferred to a slave ship. He was in love with a girl in London and decided he would go back to her a rich man. The slave trade was the best way to get rich.

The slaves were treated badly. They were kidnapped in Africa and put on slats in the hold. Sometimes, there were so many that they made them lie on their sides like spoons. They would be like this for the entire journey to what was called "The New World." Once in awhile, to clean them, they were hosed off.

However, things were not good for John. He became the servant of a slave trader in Sierra Leone. There, he was taught to brand slaves without blinking an eye. But then he grew ill himself. He was put outside on a board with a mat and a log for a pillow. His lips cracked from thirst and his stomach growled from hunger. He realized that he too had become a slave!

In 1748, a friend of his father's rescued John. He still mocked the Lord but after a time became captain of his own slave ship. That was then things began to change.

The change in John began when a terrible storm struck his ship. The waves were monsters that threatened to kill all of them on board the ship. The ship bucked and plunged through the heavy seas. All John's skill was not going to save him this time. Surely, the ship was going to sink? Winds howled around them while waves battered the vessel. Just when it seemed like all hope was gone, John lifted his voice and cried, "Lord, have mercy on us."

Later in his cabin, he thought, "Did I really call upon God? Was that why the storm calmed?"

He would always look back on that day as the day of his salvation. He still ran a slave ship for a while but he treated them as human beings, not as animals.

In 1750, John married the girl he had dreamed about for so many years and in 1755, he gave up seafaring. In fact, he fought against the evils of the slave trade with all his might until he died. In the end John Newton travelled the world but his real mission work was done from his own home. He became the pastor of a church in England and worked tirelessly to free the African people he had helped to enslave all those years before.

John Newton wrote at least 280 hymns. He was used to bring a great many people to faith in Jesus Christ. Do you know the hymn "Amazing Grace, how sweet the sound that saved a wretch like me. I once was lost but now am found, was blind but now I see." John Newton wrote it. Therefore, you see, no one can sin so much that God cannot save him. The Apostle Paul said it best in these words: *"This is a faithful saying, and worthy of all acceptance, that Christ Jesus came into the world to save sinners; of whom I am chief"* (1 Timothy 1:15).

# The Prince of Preachers

His name was Charles Haddon Spurgeon. He was a British Baptist minister that preached to as many as 6,000 people at once in the Metropolitan Tabernacle in London. He was nineteen when he began his ministry and continued until his death in 1895. He was just fifty-seven years old when he went to be with the Lord.

Other ministers hungered to read his sermons, which were widely published. They are still in print today and read by many people.

Yet, Spurgeon spoke of heartache, of having to prepare sermons and go on preaching Sunday after Sunday while people still turned away from the truth of the Gospel.

You see when you are broken-hearted, you can turn to a friend, your parents, or some other person you love and trust. It is different with preachers and the more famous you are as a preacher the harder it is. People often look at successful preachers and think that they never have problems. Therefore, the preacher feels locked up with heartbreak and sorrow that he can share only with the Lord. In fact, I have been told more than once that Spurgeon would sometimes leap from the very top of wonder and glory into the pit of despair and depression.

Never forget that people in ministry are only human with all the emotions and feelings everyone else has. Therefore, if we talk about them or hurt them in some way, they feel pain just as we would.

Spurgeon went right on preaching great sermons in spite of criticism, and accusations. It seems like the greater you are the more you are talked about and criticized. This is what Spurgeon lived with yet he never changed. He went right on serving God.

He was given the gift of public speaking. It was easy for him. All of Spurgeon's problems through the ages have helped other preachers when they have gone through the same trials. They look to the man called Spurgeon, read his sermons, and know they can go on preaching too. Therefore, Spurgeon is still speaking to us today through his writings. He preached 600 sermons before he was twenty. In fact, 20,000 of his sermons were sold every week and translated into twenty different languages. People grabbed and read them as if his words gave life and hope.

Not everyone scorned him. Multitudes waited breathlessly for the next sermon to be published. Spurgeon was called "The Prince of Preachers" since no man could preach like Charles Spurgeon. His sermons filled sixty-three books.

He was a powerful preacher yet he made his sermons clear enough that anyone could understand. His son said that sometimes he was witty and always loving.

Every week, people came to Christ through his written sermons. Spurgeon wept over lost souls and his one desire was to win the lost to Christ.

When Spurgeon was preaching to more than 10,000 people at the Music Hall of the Royal

Surrey Gardens, tragedy struck with a savage blow. Someone yelled, "FIRE" and panic took over. In the stampede to escape the flames, seven people were killed. Many think this was the cause for Spurgeon's terrible sorrow and the depression. Some even wondered if that was the cause of his early death. Sometimes, he would weep for hours yet not know why he was crying.

Another sorrow was that his wife could not have children after their twin boys were born. On top of that Spurgeon suffered endlessly with gout, joint pain, and kidney disease.

Do you think that preachers have it easy? Listen to this — Spurgeon had to care for his orphanage, the many new Christians, write 500 letters a week, talk to others about personal problems, and prepare sermons for his

4,000-member church. He could only do all that with the help of the Holy Spirit.

Once he said, "No one knows the toil and care I have to bear…". On his 50th birthday, someone read a list of sixty-six organizations he had founded. He sacrificed himself in ministry for others, all for the sake of winning souls to Christ.

This is just a little of the life of a great man called Charles Haddon Spurgeon. Spurgeon died in 1892 after writing 3,560 sermons. When I think of him, I think of the Apostle Paul, who also passed through many great trials.

*"Most gladly therefore will I rather glory in my infirmities, that the power of Christ may rest upon me" (2 Corinthians 12:9).*

# When the Fire Fell

Evan Roberts was born in Wales in 1876. From the age of twelve, he longed for God to waken his native land with revival. He longed for the people to love God with all their hearts. He longed for the churches to be full of people praising God. Evan wanted the country of Wales to be on fire for God! He carried this burden for eleven years and would stay up all night studying, praying, and weeping over his country. "Wales must have revival."

He worked in the coalmines but people said he walked in the "heavenlies". Unashamed, he took his Bible with him everywhere.

His landlady thought he was possessed of evil spirits and threw him out. He went to preaching school but the Holy Spirit urged him to leave his studies and in 1904, Evan was sent to the village of Loughor.

Sudden revival fires were sent from heaven. It was as if the people had been set alight - they were so in love with God and his word. The gospel meetings were held in a large hall with a balcony. The meetings had no order to them but at the same time there was complete order.

Bursts of praise rang out in the balcony. Songs began on the lower floor. Someone shouted that they had just given their heart to Christ. Prayer ended in song and then a testimony was given. Faces were aglow with heaven's wonder.

Evan Roberts did not preach but simply watched in wonder as the Holy Spirit led the meetings. Evan had for eleven years given himself in prayer pleading that God would do a mighty work in Wales. In his Bible he wrote, "If we seek and keep on seeking, we would find." It was as simple as that.

Sometimes, families would sit down to supper as normal. They would be eating and chatting then suddenly, everything would grow still. Someone would whisper, "Jesus," and the presence of the Holy Spirit would fall around them like a gentle rain. The meetings would go on for hours yet the men and women were strengthened by God's Spirit. In the early hours, the men would get out of bed and head out to the coalmines. Yet, the meeting halls were jammed night after night as revival fire swept the nation of Wales.

Unbelievers scorned God and the revival. New Christians however gave up their sinful ways. They had a thrilling relationship with Christ as their Saviour. They rejoiced in the mighty presence of the Holy Spirit.

Other ministers were being revived by God. One man, Seth Joshua, said in his diary, "I have never seen the power of the Holy Spirit so powerfully manifested among the people at this time."

Coalmines became churches where men worshipped God. The bars and pubs were shut down. Now, God was being honoured.

Being so mightily used and honoured of God and His works however had its price. Mark 8:34

says, "If anyone would come after me, he must deny himself and take up his cross and follow me. For whoever wants to save his life will lose it but whoever wants to lose his life for me and the gospel shall save it."

With Evan Roberts, this was the way it was. He had been a man who loved God and for years had prayed for revival. After six months of this wonderful work of God in Wales, he was a broken man, emotionally and physically. There really is a cost in carrying the cross of Christ.

A woman by the name of Mrs. Jessie Penn Lewis took him into her home, thinking a week's rest would cure him. However, he did not return to public life for almost twenty-five years, not even for his own mother's funeral.

Why do you think Jesus so often chooses the poor, the humble, and those who often have little or no education? Just look at David, the shepherd boy, or Elisha the farmer, or Peter, the fisherman? Do you suppose it was because when God moved in great ways, these men could not give themselves the credit?

*"But God has chosen the foolish things of the world to confound the wise … that no flesh should glory in his presence" (1 Corinthians 1:27, 29)*

# Apostle to the Indians

In 1785, revival came to a place called Northhampton. Churches were crowded, tears streamed down hard faces, and to the people, the Bible seemed like a new book. Bars were closed and people met even on the streets to rejoice in their salvation.

The Holy Spirit was the power behind this amazing work but the man he used was a fiery gentleman named Jonathan Edwards.

About this same time, a young man named David Brainerd was preaching the Good News of salvation to the Indians. He was called the Apostle to the Indians of America.

However, David did not have very much success. The Indians would rather have their "fire water" (whiskey). David's health began to suffer and he was forced to give up his work.

He met, fell in love with, and married the daughter of Jonathan Edwards. He, even for a time, was the pastor of a church. The salary was very good and the people were kind. The poor, tattered Indians would simply have to take care of themselves. He was now living a life of wealth and comfort, except their poor, pitiful cries haunted him. They were a people without hope and without the knowledge of Jesus dying on the cross for their sins. They were living in sin and without hope of heaven. Day and night, he struggled alone with this terrible problem. Would it be a life of comfort and ease or would it be a life of poverty for Christ?

*"But seek ye first the kingdom of God, and his righteousness; and all these things shall be added unto you. Take therefore no thought for the morrow..." (Matthew 6:33, 34).*

David had struggled and his decision was made. He resigned his church and gave up his life of ease. The Indians' pitiful cries still rang in his heart and he must obey.

Going back into the wilderness, David went from place to place to preach to his poor Indians. His travels covered more than 3,000 miles, through forest, over dangerous mountains, through fierce rains, and freezing cold. Sometimes, he was forced to sleep on a bed of snow. Entire nights were spent in prayer in the black woods as wolves howled through the bitterly cold nights.

David's first congregation was four women and a few children. As time went on, David realized that it was only through the mighty power of God's Spirit that hardened hearts could be changed. He prayed harder than ever. It is said that, "whole nights were given to pleading, earnest prayer, alone in the dark woods, with his clothes drenched in sweat."

Suddenly, the Spirit was poured upon the whole region of the Susquehanna. Indians would grasp the bridle of his horse and beg him to tell them the way of salvation. They fell at his feet in agony of soul. They gave up the "fire water" with gladness, now that the love for Christ filled their hearts.

However, the harsh winters, poor clothing, and poor bedding had its way and David became very ill with tuberculosis. Revival had come in a wonderful way but Brainerd died at the young age of twenty-seven.

*"In my Father's house are many mansions: if it were not so, I would have told you. I go to prepare a place for you" (John 14:2).*

# He Sang me to Christ

He was born in North Dakota. With the stars shining overhead, his newborn cry came from inside a tepee made of animal skins. His name was Teyet Tatonka White Feather Ramar. He would later be known as Chief White Feather. He was one of the remaining nineteen Indian chiefs left in the United States.

Someone discovered that he had a powerful and beautiful voice that could stir the hearts of people.

Leaving the reservation, he went to study music. He studied both Grand and Metropolitan opera in the United States and Milan, Italy. Everywhere he went, the crowds came to hear this Chief of the Dakota and Minnetonka Indians. He was a success and the world gladly received him. His voice soared to the rafters and touched the hearts of all that heard him.

Though he was enjoying the popularity of the world, Chief White Feather went back to his hotel at night where he felt emptiness in his heart. Even with everything the world could offer him, he was not satisfied.

Chief White Feather married a white woman. Perhaps what he needed was a mate. In time, he took her to the reservation where he had grown up. He was proud of her and eager to show her off to his people but when she saw the way his people lived, she was horrified and left him.

Chief White Feather was shattered. Now he was emptier and more alone than ever. It was the one great heartbreak of his life. The world, wealth, and fame meant nothing to him.

In his despair, he found the Lord Jesus Christ and surrendered his life to Him. He left the success of the opera and began following the Lord in Gospel music. Instead of losing his wonderful voice, it grew richer, stronger and better in every way. He travelled around the world, going to every church that invited him, whether small or large.

Another woman, too, had emptiness in her heart that nothing could fill. Betty was only a teenager, but she was a sinful teenager in need of the Saviour. Though her parents had once walked with God, she knew nothing about Jesus. This young girl had no idea that Jesus could fill the emptiness of her heart.

One evening, Betty's mom was reading the newspaper and said, "I see that an Indian Chief is coming to the Baptist church. You know, I think I'll go hear him."

Betty was surprised to hear herself say, "I think I'll go too."

Betty's dad drove them to the church and all three of them sat down to listen to Chief White Feather.

The church was small and seemed to be filled with breathless wonder. The most amazing figure stepped out onto the platform. He wore beaded moccasins and a full-feathered headdress came from the top of his head all the way down to his feet.

He began to sing. Betty had never heard such a wonderful voice. Tears streamed down her face as Chief White Feather sang, "I'd rather have

Jesus than silver and gold, I'd rather have Jesus than riches untold... ."

That was the night Betty's life was turned upside down for that night she gave her heart to the Lord Jesus Christ.

Perhaps I should say, "That was the night that I gave my heart to the Lord Jesus," for Betty is actually me. The other good thing is that my mom and dad also came back to the Lord that night.

Somehow, we became close friends with Chief White Feather and he stayed in our home many times when he was preaching and singing in the area where we lived. Just think, when Chief White Feather sang, "I'd rather have Jesus" he knew exactly what he was singing about. He knew what the song meant. He knew that having Jesus is better than having anything else that the world can offer.

Sometimes the devil knocks us down and it might look as though we've been destroyed. However, the Bible says, *"...you thought evil against me, but God meant it for good"* *(Genesis 50:20).* The devil tried to destroy Chief White Feather in robbing him of his wife, but God used the Chief's heartache to bring many people to Jesus.

We can be knocked down and saddened in some way, but it is only the one who stays down that is defeated. God has called us to be victorious. So what do we do? We get up again and let Him use us. It is hard, but God always uses broken things such as the expensive jar of perfume that was poured on Jesus' head or the fish and bread that Jesus broke to feed the multitude. He especially uses hearts that have been broken.

Because Chief White Feather got up after being broken, me, and many others like me are a part of the family of God today. Remember, "I'd still rather have Jesus!"

# Today's Martyrs

Do you think that today's missionaries have it easy, without terrible things happening to them? Some do but before we begin this story read the 11th chapter of Hebrews. In this chapter we read about some people who had victories. However, as you keep reading, you will discover two little words that change everything - the words "and others". The "and others" refers to people that were tortured just because they believed in Jesus. Some were killed, and some hid in caves and dressed in animal skins. Do you know what God said about this second group of people? He said the world was not worthy of them.

Recently in India there were two people who had just become Christians. Manrathan and his wife lived in a village where Christians were hated. But Manrathan became a preacher of the gospel and in spite of the hatred of Christians he and his wife built a church and God blessed them. They held a special service so that new Christians could tell others about Jesus Christ and his love. Someone became a Christian and soon the news was spreading all over the area.

Now India is a Hindu country where many gods are worshipped. To become a Christian and deny all other gods is very serious. It can be dangerous for people when they make a decision to follow Christ.

Soon in Manrathan's village a great mob gathered and walked towards the small church. They began beating the Christians. Manrathan, his wife, and a Bible woman named Sarita were taken prisoner and tied to what they called the "sacred tree" where they were severely beaten.

All they could do was trust in an all-powerful God. There were no policemen to come and help them. Their only hope was Jesus.

No one was allowed to leave the village, for the mob did not want anyone to learn of the beatings. However, one believer did manage to get away and told what was happening in his village.

Manrathan's captors demanded 25,000 rupees as ransom because they felt the village had been dishonoured by the preaching of the Gospel. That kind of money was huge and something the Christians did not have. However, if the money was not paid within 48 hours, the prisoners would be killed.

Manrathan, his wife and Sarita knew their captors were not kidding. The same people had burned to death an Australian missionary, Graham Staines, and his two children some years before. In addition, a number of native missionaries had been murdered as well. The Gospel was not welcome in the villages! Was there any hope for these three Christians? It certainly did not look that way.

However, as word of their capture and torture began to spread, Christians began to pray earnestly for their release. It seemed unlikely that such a vicious mob would let their prisoners go without being paid the large sum of money. Yet, as Christians everywhere continued to pray, a miracle happened and they were released.

This story happened on September 10, 2004. Manrathan, his wife and Sarita have been slowly recovering from their injuries. Has this stopped missionary work in India? Far from it! In fact, 14,000 native missionaries face torture and death every day of their lives as they continue to boldly preach the word of God. Because of their sacrifice, ten new churches are being formed in Asia every single day!

*"And let us not be weary in well doing: for in due season we shall reap, if we faint not"* (Galatians 6:9).

# Missionary Stories from Around the World Quiz

1. What is the meaning of the name of Indian tribe, 'Aucas'?

2. Which scripture did Elisabeth Elliot hold on to when she went back to the Auca village following the death of her husband?

3. At what age did Robert Moffat give his heart to Jesus?

4. How many 'temple' children did Amy Carmichael rescue?

5. How many years did William Carey serve God in India before he saw his first convert?

6. What did Gladys Pierson do when she could not get out of her bed after her fall?

7. Which countries were at war when Gladys Aylward went to China as a missionary?

8. Hudson Taylor read a Gospel tract entitled 'It is Finished.' What did he learn from it?

9. What did Isobel Kuhn do when she was afraid?

10. Which was more important to Lottie Moon, to obey man or God?

11. How was an accident avoided when the brakes did not work on the vehicle in which Mr & Mrs Schmidt were travelling?

12. How did God tell Lillian Trasher he wanted her to serve in Egypt?

13. What did Tak'ke do when he was captured?

14. What did Bob Pruett and Ernie Rebb find the Pygmies doing when they visited them on their second trip into the bush country of the Philippine Islands?

15. How many people in the witch doctor's village came to Jesus after he did?

16. What did Justin Buckamye do when the man-eating lion came to the village church in the African jungle?

17. What burden did God place on the hearts of friends of Mr & Mrs Jackson when they were in Mau Mau country?

18. How many years did the people in the village wait for a white man to come and teach them about the Jesus tribe?

19. How did Mary Slessor get the courage to face up to the savages she worked amongst?

20. What were the famous words Henry Stanley said to David Livingstone when he found him in Tanganyika?

21. The soldiers wanted Julio and Juan to deny Jesus Christ and stop preaching the gospel. What happened when they refused?

22. Can you name one of the famous hymns that John Newton wrote?

23. How many sermons did Charles Haddon Spurgeon preach before the age of twenty?

24. How many years did Evan Roberts pray for a move of God in Wales?

25. Who was known as the 'Apostle to the Indians'?

26. What song did Chief White Feather sing the night Betty gave her heart to Jesus?

27. What can we do to help people who are tortured for their faith in Jesus Christ today?

# Answers

1. Savage.

2. 'I do not fear what man can do unto me. The Lord is on my side to help me.'

3. Four.

4. 1000.

5. Seven years.

6. She searched the Bible looking for the answer.

7. China and Russia.

8. He learnt what Christ's death was about and why sins were paid for by His blood. His death finished the work of salvation.

9. She spoke to God in prayer.

10. To obey God.

11. Because Mom Keymer felt the need to pray for them.

12. Through the reading of her Bible.

13. He called on the Lord to help him.

14. They we praying and singing while celebrating the death and resurrection of Jesus.

15. The entire village.

16. He remembered Daniel in the lion's den and that God's power is just the same today. He told the people not to fear for 'The God of Daniel is with us.'

17. They were burdened to pray for them.

18. Twenty years.

19. Only by the grace of God.

20. 'Dr Livingstone, I presume?'

21. Julio was shot and Juan prayed for his enemies. Afterwards they all became Christians because of the testimony of the two men.

22. 'Amazing Grace'.

23. 600.

24. Eleven years.

25. David Brainerd.

26. 'I'd rather have Jesus than silver or gold, I'd rather have him than have riches untold.'

27. Pray for them.

**CHRISTIAN FOCUS PUBLICATIONS**

Christian Focus | Christian Heritage | CF4K | Mentor

Christian Focus Publications publishes books for adults and children under its four main imprints: Christian Focus, CF4K, Mentor and Christian Heritage. Our books reflect our conviction that God's Word is reliable and Jesus is the way to know him, and live for ever with him.

Our children's publication list includes a Sunday School curriculum that covers pre-school to early teens, and puzzle and activity books. We also publish personal and family devotional titles, biographies and inspirational stories that children will love.

If you are looking for quality Bible teaching for children then we have an excellent range of Bible stories and age-specific theological books.

From pre-school board books to teenage apologetics, we have it covered!

## Find us at our web page:
## www.christianfocus.com

CF4•K
Because you're never
too young to know Jesus